do it right!

THE NEW BOOK OF BUSINESS ETIQUETTE

do it right!

THE NEW BOOK OF BUSINESS ETIQUETTE

CornerStone Leadership Institute
P.O. Box 764087
Dallas, TX 75376
888.789.LEAD

Printed in the United States of America
ISBN: 0-9788137-8-2

Credits

Design, art direction, and production — Melissa Monogue, Back Porch Creative, Plano, TX
info@BackPorchCreative.com

Copy Editor — Kathleen Green, Positively Proofed, Plano, TX
info@PositivelyProofed.com

Foreword

BY LETITIA BALDRIDGE

Valerie Sokolosky is a courageous front lines fighter for civility in the workplace. As a fellow observer of the role that manners play in the conduct of successful business, I'm sure she agrees that it has become more noticeable with every passing decade that our society is in trouble. We're not as nice as we used to be, nor as caring, observant and kind. People skills are more important than ever in business. We need to stop and think – about how our children are growing up, how our managers are treating our customers, how our employees are "getting along" with one another. How can we improve our conversation? How can we communicate better?

To borrow from a song title, people really do need people. And manners make any group of people somehow work together just fine. Knowing how to behave makes life worth living, and makes society go forward instead of into reverse gear.

Letitia Baldridge
Social Secretary to the White House,
Chief of Staff for Jacqueline Kennedy
and author of many business etiquette books

Beginning at the Beginning

We've all had them – those uncomfortable moments at business meetings, on the telephone, during a business lunch or in the middle of an interview. "What's the right thing to do?" we wonder. "What's socially or politically correct?"

We are living in a time of etiquette ambiguity. What was once the behavioral norm has disappeared. Today we're often forced to make it up as we go.

By reading and applying the information on these pages, you will get answers for those gray areas, such as:

- Should I stand when a senior executive enters a room?
- How do I recover from a faux pas like mispronouncing someone's name?
- How can I network at a large business event when I know absolutely no one?
- What does business casual look like?
- When should I bcc: someone?
- What do I say when someone pays me a compliment?
- When I'm traveling internationally, what kinds of things should I know?

And much more.

Take these tips on business trips, to meetings, interviews and presentations. It's the perfect refresher course to browse through on the plane while traveling to that important conference.

What do you do? What do you say? When are you out of line? When are you on target? You'll never have to guess again.

Read *Do It Right!* today and watch your career take giant steps forward!

Table of Contents

IN THE OFFICE

"Arrogance is attitudinal.
Check it at the door."
– Benjamin Franklin

Business protocol is to the business world what gasoline is to the automobile.

- ✦ It powers relationships.
- ✦ It drives cooperation.
- ✦ It fuels communication.

Business protocol also smoothes out the rough spots on our highway to success.

- ✦ Graciousness overcomes growling.
- ✦ Encouragement diminishes insults.
- ✦ Kindness replaces crudeness.
- ✦ Growth challenges groans.

What most employees only glance over during their first week on the job is actually the silent engine of the organization. If you haven't reviewed your organization's protocols – a guideline describing correct etiquette and procedures – now's the time.

Not only are these protocols internally powerful, they are equally powerful in business-to-business, community and employee relationships. Remember, your organization's image is based on those representing it.

People never intentionally exhibit poor etiquette. Most of the time, they simply do not know. This handbook will provide you and your team the information needed to conduct business with class, style and presence.

1

Top Ten Tips for Every Employee:

- Be accountable and responsible.
- Be timely and truthful.
- Use technology only for business during work.
- Never gossip or become part of the rumor mill.
- Don't violate others' personal and private space.
- Know when to comment, when to listen.
- Give what's needed (extra energy and effort) when needed.
- When you have the experience, volunteer for an opportunity to show your leadership.
- Respect decisions made by the boss.
- Show up – be there in the moment.

2 Knowledge breeds confidence. Educate your team on organizational culture as well as the rules of etiquette. Eliminate as many of etiquette's unknowns as possible.

3 When attending an event hosted by another company, it's not the time to gain sales opportunities by handing the guests your business cards.

4 One simple rule about office parties and business festivities: No matter what the occasion, it's still business, and moderation works best.

5 Stay positive. Leave your moods at home.

6 **Be a time saver, not a time waster!**

- ✦ Plan your work – then work your plan.
- ✦ Stay off the phone and Internet, except for necessary business.
- ✦ Keep breaks and lunch to the designated time frame.
- ✦ Save personal reading for personal time.

7 When you are given information in confidence, keep that confidence.

8 Respect the other person's time. Choose your words carefully, stay focused on the topic and make every word count.

9 Respect privacy of a co-worker's cubicle or office. Carry on conversations in your own space.

10 Don't live in a WAM (What About Me!) world. Try this exercise: Go one day in the office without saying "I." Say "we" instead, e.g., instead of saying, "I need that report today," say "We need that report today." Business is, in fact, not always about you.

11 **Aim. Don't blame. Take action. Don't complain.**

- Aim at a solution instead of blaming someone else.
- Listen to suggestions, offer your input and be part of the solution.
- Get on board and support decisions after they are made.

12 Etiquette does not depend on gender. Men and women should treat each other equally. Equal treatment means:

- Whoever gets to the door first, open it!
- For revolving doors, offer to lead the way.
- When someone is struggling with a coat, give assistance.
- Men and women are equally responsible for picking up the tab.

13 If you're sitting in someone's office and they take a phone call, unless they indicate for you to stay seated, stand up and offer to wait outside until the conversation has ended.

14 **When you receive a job performance evaluation:**

- Consider the evaluation not as a report card but as a learning tool.
- Reflect on all that is said before you comment or ask questions.
- Politely discuss areas in the appraisal you think need clarification.

- Stay positive.
- Come to a mutual understanding before ending the conversation.

15 If during an evaluation or an interview for a promotion you are asked about the salary you desire, respond by saying, "I expect the fair market value. Maybe you can tell me your range."

16 Communicate with a K. I. S. S. – Keep It Short and Simple!

17 **Little things count:**

- Positive attitude
- Appreciation
- Open and direct communication
- Please and thank you

18 Treat everyone with respect, regardless of their position.

19 We expect praise from our bosses, but we should also give praise for their outstanding efforts. Bosses need recognition, too.

20 Stand when someone enters your office for the first time and greet them. Stand when shaking hands or making introductions.

21 Refer to those with advanced medical degrees as Doctor [last name], unless they invite you to use their first name.

22 When in doubt, Mr. or Ms. is always correct.

23 In an academic setting, it is correct to refer to someone as "Doctor" if they have earned a doctorate degree. You may also call them "Professor." In settings outside academia, Mr. or Ms. is appropriate.

24 **Common courtesies at the office:**

- ✦ When office hours are 9-to-5, this means work starts at 9.
- ✦ Never criticize anyone in front of others.
- ✦ "Open door" doesn't mean walk in anytime without permission.
- ✦ Don't eat at your desk. Eat food over a table, not the phone.

25 Foul language stinks. Using bathroom talk can flush your business down the toilet.

26 **When a client visits:**

- ✦ Have clear objectives in mind for the meeting.
- ✦ Have open-ended questions ready to glean information.
- ✦ Anticipate comments and questions and be ready to respond.
- ✦ Take time to clear the clutter and organize yourself.
- ✦ Look at the person speaking.
- ✦ Listen.
- ✦ Ask questions.
- ✦ At the end of the meeting, repeat the points you have heard. Then take action on what you've promised.

27 Etiquette based on adapting to the other person's style makes good business sense. Do unto others as they would have you do unto them … and would do unto you.

28 **Save terms of endearment for those who are dear:**

- "Honey" is something you spread on toast.
- A "Hun" is a warrior who followed Attila.
- A "deer" is an animal in the forest.
- A "girl" is any female under age 12 … not a secretary or assistant.

None of these work in business.

"If you make the obvious effort to be accommodating, sympathetic and kind, business will transpire, and deals will be made … and profits and goals will be realized."

– Letitia Baldridge

BUSINESS LUNCHEONS, RECEPTIONS AND ENTERTAINING

"Class is learned and earned."

Business etiquette inspires in the office what table manners inspire in the family.

Remember sitting at the dining-room table and eating a holiday meal as a parent carefully monitored your every move? Did you remember to put your napkin in your lap? Did you forget and put your elbows on the table or chew with your mouth open? Undoubtedly, any slip in table manners would be dealt with after the guests had gone home.

Those stern looks your mother or father shot across the table, however, were actually preparing you for your career in the business world. The values you learned, even the most painful of those lessons, instilled tools that were destined to help you attain success in your business relationships – civility, harmony, acceptance and respect.

How often do these tools come in handy as you negotiate a deal or mediate a disagreement? How many times has the ability to accept reality or a final judgment allowed you to move seamlessly to the next project? When have these and other tools made it possible for you to enter a new arena of self-confidence, feeling equipped to do what you do best?

Business entertaining is often a requirement to achieve one or more of the following objectives:

- Form relationships.
- Express gratitude for previous business.
- Celebrate and reward business success.
- Create an atmosphere for decision-making away from the office.

Knowing and practicing the etiquette of entertaining becomes a valuable business tool for every member of your team. Use your experiences to mentor others.

29

Top Ten Tips for Attending Business Meals:

- Arrive promptly and remain standing until the host indicates where you should sit.
- Place your napkin in your lap as soon as you are seated.
- Never order the most expensive item on the menu. Avoid

ordering hard-to-handle foods when trying to make a positive first impression, e.g., spaghetti, barbecue ribs, onion soup.

- ✦ Start eating when your host begins eating.
- ✦ Don't know which is yours and which belongs to the person sitting next to you? Remember "BMW" – the Bread plate is on your left, the Main plate is in front of you and your Water glass is on the right of your plate.
- ✦ If you use a packaged sweetener, tear off only a corner, and place the empty container on the table, just under the edge of your bread plate.
- ✦ Never salt your food before tasting it first. Salt and pepper are always passed together, even if someone asks for one.
- ✦ Pass food counterclockwise around the table the first serving. Then pass food to the person requesting it in the shortest route.
- ✦ If you eat an olive with a pit or find gristle, bone or other things in your food, quickly remove it from your mouth and place it on the side of your plate.
- ✦ Place your napkin on the chair if you leave the table during the meal. Your napkin stays in your lap until everyone is ready to leave the table. Then place it, folded, to the left of your plate.

30 **"Always" rules for savvy hosts at business events:**

- ✦ Invite a variety of personalities and business types.
- ✦ Extend invitations in plenty of time – about two to three weeks ahead.
- ✦ Treat every guest as a V.I.P.
- ✦ Never make issue of a mistake, such as accidental spills or misuse of silverware.
- ✦ Watch alcohol intake. People are watching your lead.
- ✦ Smile. Mingle. Visit. Introduce. Put your guests at ease.

31 **When hosting a reception:**

- Reserve only for special occasions – retirements, anniversaries, opening nights!
- Hold your event between 6:00 and 8:00 p.m. or 10:30 p.m. and midnight, depending on regional preferences.
- A reception is not a place for lengthy discussion. The idea is to mix and mingle socially with many people.

32 **Plan entertaining thoroughly, carefully and well in advance.**

- If your budget allows, a meeting planner or staff assistant can save wear and tear … on you!
- Consider how to best facilitate business objectives. Plan for sufficient room and privacy with plenty of comfortable seating.
- Have good food and adequate service staff in the kitchen.
- If you must cut down on expenses, invite fewer guests. Never sacrifice quality for quantity.

33 **Initiate introductions. Don't wait. Just do it!**

- When introducing yourself to strangers, relax. They are probably feeling uncomfortable, as well, and will be delighted you took the initiative to make the introduction.
- When introducing someone to your client, mention the client's name first. "Mr. Client, I'd like you to meet my boss, Bill Jones."
- When introducing a person into a group, mention that person's name first. "Paul, I'd like you to meet my friends."

33 **When a business breakfast is effective:**

- When you know the person's best alert time is in the morning.

- To brainstorm when everyone is fresh at the day's beginning.
- When there are few issues to discuss.
- To introduce a new employee.
- To discuss an upcoming meeting or event.
- To tie up loose ends.

35 When a business lunch is effective:

- To get to know someone more personally.
- As a first meeting with a client.
- During the interview process.
- To discuss a proposal or plan of action.

36 When a business dinner is appropriate:

- To entertain out-of-town business associates.
- As a special acknowledgment for a job well done or other recognition.
- As an opportunity to invite spouses.
- To keep the time frame open-ended, so no one feels rushed.

37 How to offer a toast:

- Never offer a toast before the host.
- When the host offers a toast to the guest of honor, raise your glass, nod your head toward the honored guest, and take a sip along with everyone else.
- If you would like to make a toast, subtly request permission from your host. Keep remarks short and positive.
- You may make or take part in a toast with a nonalcoholic beverage.

- When you are the guest of honor, acknowledge the host's toast with a smile (do not raise your glass). You may extend a toast to him in return.

38 **Awkward situation? Don't know what to do?**

- Someone uses your bread and butter plate? Put your bread on your dinner plate.
- Someone drinks out of your water glass? Order tea.
- Someone has had too much to drink? Help remove them from the situation.
- You're trying to have a conversation while sitting next to people who are talking too loud? Suggest moving to another table or finish the discussion at a later time.

39 In countries where food is at a premium, leaving food on your plate is considered bad manners. In America, feel free to leave some food on your plate since our servings are often super-sized helpings.

40 **If you're conducting business during a meal:**

- Start with casual conversation.
- Turn the conversation gradually to business, but begin before dessert! Say, "I appreciate you taking time away from the office so that we can discuss …."

41 When attending a business buffet, the best etiquette is not to pile your plate high. Take only what you'll eat. You can go back for second helpings.

42 **Eight tips for eating while standing:**

- ✦ Assume food served without utensils is finger food.
- ✦ When standing, balance your drink and your plate of food in your left hand with your cocktail napkin under the plate for easy wiping.
- ✦ Since people are more conscious of germs today, you might move your plate to your right hand to eat with your left after shaking hands.
- ✦ Place a napkin under your glass when setting it down.
- ✦ Enjoy the foods you can eat. Don't discuss those you can't.
- ✦ Mingle. Avoid monopolizing anyone's attention.
- ✦ Accept refreshments, even if you do not eat or drink them.
- ✦ Never feel awkward asking for a nonalcoholic drink.

43 To leave one group of people and move to another at an event or reception graciously, simply say, "Excuse me. I've enjoyed talking with you." Then walk away.

44 **When the party's over:**

- ✦ Thank the host for the invitation.
- ✦ Compliment the host/hostess on the party.
- ✦ Leave just a bit before the appointed hour.
- ✦ Send a handwritten, thank-you note within one to two days.

45 **Be a good guest when you receive an invitation:**

- ✦ RSVP – these four little words remain a mystery for many. However, when you receive an invitation asking for an RSVP (from the French – *respondez sil vous plait* – which means "please respond") simply call or e-mail the host to say whether or not you plan to attend.

- Respond quickly – one week maximum!
- Can't attend at the last minute? Don't earn the reputation of a "no-show." Call your host before the event. In the rare case you are not able to attend, call the next day to apologize.

46 **For smooth entertaining, understand the restaurant service staff and their functions:**

- Maitre d' – the headwaiter who leads you to your table.
- Captain – the waiter who takes your order and supervises your meal service.
- Wine steward – the expert (often called "sommelier") who can guide your wine selection.
- Waiter – your server.

47 **Knowing when and how much to tip is imperative:**

- Good service equals a good tip. Don't be cheap when the service is outstanding. These minimums are courtesy of the American Society of Travel Agents.
    - Parking attendant – $1 to $2
    - Valet – $2 to $5
    - Taxi or limo driver – 15%
    - Waiter/waitress – 15% to 20% (excluding tax)
    - Wine steward or sommelier – $3 to $5 per bottle
    - Bartender – 15% to 20%
    - Hotel bellman – $1 per bag
    - Doorman hailing a taxi – $1
    - Concierge – $2 to $10
    - Cloakroom attendants – $1 per coat

TIPS FOR SAVVY LEADERS

*"Treat people as if they were what
they ought to be and you help them
to become what they are capable of being."*
– Johann W. von Goethe

The successful business plan places business etiquette as its first priority. Put your people before the program!

When John Robinson inherited his sales team, he was told he had the best group of people in the company. In his first team meeting, he set goals for the group – some of the highest in the department – and then supported each team member throughout the quarter.

When the results were tabulated at the end of the year, John's team had exceeded the best team performance in company history.

At the conclusion of the annual sales meeting, the vice president of sales pulled John aside. "When we gave you this group, we weren't sure how things would go," he said.

John looked puzzled. "We had all classified this team as a bunch of losers," the VP continued. "They hadn't done well for months and all were on the verge of being fired … until you were promoted. Because we told you they were the best – and you believed they were the best – they lived up to that. Because you expected successful performances from each one, they lived up to your expectation … and finally began to tap into their individual potential."

John smiled at the irony, for as he had taken the reins of the new team, he wasn't sure whether he had what it took to become a leader. His company's experiment had solidified his leadership role and paved his way into top management.

"Unless he manages himself effectively,
no amount of ability, skill, experience
or knowledge will make an executive effective."

– Peter Drucker

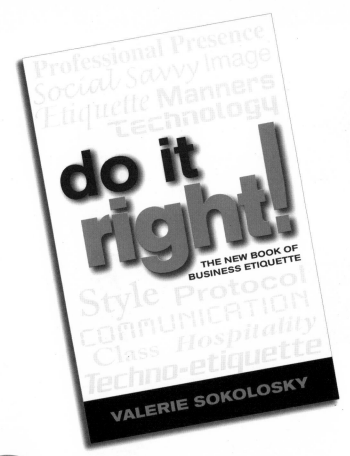

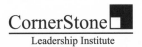

Accelerate Personal G

12 Choices...That Lead to Your Success is about success – how to achieve it, keep it and enjoy it – by making better choices. **$14.95**

Too Many Emails contains dozens of tips and techniques to increase your email effectiveness and efficiency. **$9.95**

Orchestrating Attitude translates the abstract into the actionable. It cuts through the clutter to deliver inspiration and application so you can orchestrate your attitude ... and your success. **$9.95**

Conquering Adversity – Six Strategies to Move You and Your Team Through Tough Times is a practical guide to help people and organizations deal with the unexpected and move forward through adversity. **$14.95**

107 Ways to Stick to It What's the REAL secret to success? Learn the secrets from the world's highest achievers. These practical tips and inspiring stories will help you stick to it and WIN! **$9.95**

The Ant and the Elephant is a different kind of book for a different kind of leader! A great story that teaches that we must lead ourselves before we can expect to be an effective leader of others. **$12.95**

175 Ways to Get More Done in Less Time has 175 really good suggestions that will help you get things done faster ... and usually better. **$9.95**

136 Effective Presentation Tips provides you with inside tips from two of the best presenters in the world. **$9.95**

th Package $139.95

Becoming the Obvious Choice is a roadmap showing each employee how they can maintain their motivation, develop their hidden talents and become the best. **$9.95**

Silver Bullets offers straightforward tips that will inspire personal and professional growth to take you to the top. **$14.95**

You and Your Network is profitable reading for those who want to learn how to develop healthy relationships with others. “I think every living person should read and re-read this book. It can change your life.” – David Cottrell
$9.95

The NEW CornerStone Perpetual Calendar, a compelling collection of quotes about leadership and life, is perfect for office desks, school and home. Offering a daily dose of inspiration, this terrific calendar makes the perfect gift or motivational reward.
$14.95

The CornerStone Leadership Collection of Cards is designed to make it easy for you to show appreciation for your team, clients and friends. The awesome photography and your personal message written inside will create a lasting impact. Pack/12 (12 styles/1 each) **$24.95**
Posters also available.

One of each of the items shown here are included in the *Accelerate Personal Growth* Package!

YES! Please send me extra copies of *Do It Right!*

1-30 copies $14.95 31-100 copies $13.95 101+ copies $12.9

Do It Right!	____ copies X ______	= $______

Additional Personal Growth Resources

Accelerate Personal Growth Package (Includes all items shown inside.)	____ pack(s) X $139.95	= $______

Other Books

______________________	____ copies X ______	= $______
______________________	____ copies X ______	= $______
______________________	____ copies X ______	= $______
______________________	____ copies X ______	= $______
______________________	____ copies X ______	= $______
	Shipping & Handling	$______
	Subtotal	$______
	Sales Tax (8.25%-TX Only)	$______
	Total (U.S. Dollars Only)	**$______**

Shipping and Handling Charges

Total $ Amount	Up to $49	$50-$99	$100-$249	$250-$1199	$1200-$2999	$3000
Charge	$6	$9	$16	$30	$80	$125

Name ______________________ Job Title ______________

Organization ______________________ Phone ______________

Shipping Address ______________________ Fax ______________

Billing Address ______________________ E-mail ______________
(required when ordering PowerPoint® Presentati

City ______________________ State ________ ZIP ________

❑ Please invoice (Orders over $200) Purchase Order Number (if applicable) ________

Charge Your Order: ❑ MasterCard ❑ Visa ❑ American Express

Credit Card Number ______________________ Exp. Date ________

Signature ______________________

❑ Check Enclosed (Payable to: CornerStone Leadership)

Fax 972.274.2884
Phone 888.789.5323

www.**CornerStoneLeadership**.com

P.O. Box 76408
Dallas, TX 7537

48 Top Ten Tips for Leaders:

- Lead by example. Always follow through with your commitment.
- Set and maintain a standard of courtesy, excellence and integrity.
- Guide, don't condemn.
- Discuss problems in private. Be sensitive to employee issues.
- Make expectations crystal clear.
- Be a mentor. Help employees advance.
- Encourage employee input.
- Commend positive performance.
- Express confidence in employees in the presence of clients.
- Show appreciation for extra effort.

49 When interviewing candidates:

- Be as prepared for the interview as your candidate. The interview is a two-way street. They're hiring you at the same time you're hiring them.
- Put the candidate at ease. Smile and remember when you were in that same position. Ask not only traditional questions related to skills and experience, but also ask behavioral questions, such as how the candidate handled a situation, e.g., "When did you recently reach a goal and how did you achieve it?" or "When did you make an unpopular decision and how did you implement it?"
- Let the candidate do the majority of the talking.
- Treat him/her with respect by showing interest in them as a job candidate and as an individual.
- Take notes while regularly maintaining eye contact.

- Keep all information discussed confidential.
- After the interview, keep the applicant informed if he/she is being considered.

50 When giving a job performance evaluation:

- Have facts to substantiate the overall evaluation.
- Express your thoughts, rationales and ideas simply and clearly.
- Reiterate the organization's priorities and anchor your comments to the team's mission.
- Reinforce the positive and redirect the negative.
- Give positive guidance and direction.
- When addressing areas that require correction, lead with specific examples of observable behaviors.
- Set an agreed upon plan for improvement, and have the employee sign it with dates for completing the actions.

51 Etiquette for meetings:

- Host should send a planned agenda distributed ahead of time along with time, objective of the meeting and expectation for outcomes or decisions to be made.
- Start and stop on time. Don't wait for latecomers.
- Meetings should be consistently focused on topics related to the overall strategies.
- Allow all participants to be involved. Create an atmosphere that encourages participation.
- Expect and encourage challenge. The goal is to generate continuous improvement at every level.

- Meetings should be followed by a distribution of minutes, citing decisions made and assignments given with targeted completion dates.

52

Read at least one book a year. You'll be in the top 15 percent of the world intellectually. Consider books on tape for commutes and other travel.

53

Keep learning. For every leader, knowledge is the mightiest tool … and only the leaders who continue learning can be the most successful. Learning is a lifetime initiative.

54

Keep your network working! A savvy leader has vast linkages to subject-matter experts, decision makers and influencers in varied fields of business.

55

Savvy leaders show respect.

- They mentor others.
- They train, educate and coach.
- They show respect for people above, subordinates and colleagues.
- They remain calm and collected in demeanor and appearance.
- They lead upward, downward and sideways.
- They recognize and build people.
- They know that people are motivated differently.

According to surveys by the Wharton Center for Applied Research, managers report that only 56% of their meetings are productive – and that 25% would have been more effective as conference calls, memos, e-mails, or voicemails. Conclusion: the cost of misguided meetings is high.

PEOPLE TO PEOPLE

"One person can make a difference and every person should try."
– John F. Kennedy

As the story goes, Dwight Morrow, the father of Anne Morrow Lindbergh, once held a dinner party to which Calvin Coolidge had been invited.

After Coolidge left, Morrow told the remaining guests that Coolidge would make a good president. The others disagreed. They felt Coolidge was too quiet, that he lacked color and personality. No one would like him, they said.

Six-year-old Anne then spoke up: "I like him," she said. Then she displayed a finger with a small bandage around it. "He was the only one at the party who asked about my sore finger."

"And that's why he would make a good president," her father added … and the rest is history.

56 **Top Ten Tips When Working With Others (Some things go without saying, but we'll say them just the same!)**

- Respect the other person's personal space – usually two feet.
- Chewing gum has no place in the work environment. It detracts from your professional image … and is annoying.
- Slang or street talk ("you guys," "cool," "sweet," "dude," etc.) has no place in a professional setting.
- Flirting isn't appropriate in the workplace. Period.
- Tapping your fingers or other nervous habits are distracting and annoying to others.
- The business environment is not a place to clip your nails or pick your nose or your teeth.
- Off-color jokes are not appreciated by most professionals.
- Speaking with food in your mouth only serves one purpose – to make others lose their appetites.
- Complete all projects efficiently and correctly.
- Being late regularly shows selfish and disrespectful behavior.

57 If you forget someone's name, begin introductions with those you do know by saying, "Do you know my friend Ellen?" This will give the person whose name you've forgotten a chance to use their name in their introduction … and, at the same time, bail you out.

58 Offer a handshake both to initiate and to complete a meeting. Proper etiquette is a firm but gentle and self-assured handshake while maintaining eye contact.

59 At a gathering where you don't know anyone, don't stand with your hands in your pockets or your arms folded. These poses communicate you are not approachable. Instead, smile and be the first one to extend your hand to the next person who passes.

60 Demonstrating "class behavior" in the business setting is often as simple as allowing others to express their ideas and opinions and appreciating those expressions.

61 Maintain a database of information on individuals with whom you want to follow up or cultivate a relationship. Knowing children's names, birthdays, anniversaries or other information helps make your follow-up personal.

62 Take care to demonstrate character – don't be one!

63 Build relationships regularly!

> ***Relationship***: The state of being mutually interested. Reverence or respect for another. To be involved, concerned.

64 **If you want to learn what a person is really like, ask three questions:**

- ✦ What makes them laugh?
- ✦ What makes them angry?
- ✦ What makes them excited?

65 Learn and grow – in any business environment:

- Learn how to learn – from others. You can't possibly know it all.
- Learn from your experiences.
- Learn quickly.
- Learn without complaint.
- Learn and share your learning with others.

66 Show respect for seniority:

- Let a senior executive precede you into a room.
- Never assume you're on a first-name basis with someone. Address them with their full titles, as Mr., Ms., Dr., etc., unless they ask you to call them by their first names.
- Stand up to greet or say goodbye. Don't take a seat until senior employees or key players have seated themselves.
- Introduce guests to your boss first.

67 When you go for an interview:

- Unless you want your wings clipped, never "wing it!" Learn all you can about the company, the business, the culture and the position in advance.
- Be prepared to share what you can do for the organization, how you can make a difference.
- Take several copies of your resume.
- Ask people beforehand if they will provide a reference letter for you.
- Make your first appointment with the decision maker whenever possible.

- Are you in sales? Contact the vice president of sales.
- Are you an executive? Contact the president.

68 Successful interview etiquette:

- ✦ Arrive 15 minutes early.
- ✦ Be courteous to the receptionist or administrative assistant.
- ✦ Give your name, appointment time and business card.
- ✦ When the interviewer ushers you into his/her office, wait for them to indicate where you are to sit – and sit tall.
- ✦ Unless the interviewer is familiar, never use first names.
- ✦ Place your materials in your lap or neatly on the floor, never on the interviewer's desk!
- ✦ Listen carefully and learn. Smile, nod occasionally and be yourself!
- ✦ Relate your qualifications and your desire to do a good job.
- ✦ Do not discuss salary or vacation time.
- ✦ Shake hands when leaving and thank them for their time.
- ✦ Send a short, handwritten thank-you note expressing appreciation for their time and how you look forward to hearing from them.

69 Respect the home-office executive:

- ✦ Never drop by without calling.
- ✦ Never abuse after-hours time.
- ✦ Never abuse weekend family time simply because the person is accessible.

70 **When you blow it, pick yourself up and go on:**

- Successful people experience failure 70 percent of the time.
- Take risks and learn from them.
- Keep at it.

71 **Execute and follow through:**

- Execution is equally as important as commitment.
- Commitment means nothing without the follow-through.
- Lack of follow-through demonstrates a lack of integrity.

72 **Show tact by:**

- Thoughtfulness toward others.
- Sensitivity to the atmosphere of the moment.
- Showing a combination of interest, sincerity and caring.

73 Communicate openly! Co-workers, your staff and clients can't read your mind. Communicate your ideas and requests clearly.

74 **Dealing with the door:**

- On elevators, those in front step out to let others exit.
- At office doors, the person arriving first should open it.
- If someone opens the door for you, say "Thank you."

75 **Know the facts to avoid making assumptions:**

- Assumption is arrogance.
- Assumption is error.
- Assumption is the mother of mistake.

76 **Sidebar conversational taboos:**

- Tasteless jokes
- Politics
- Religion
- Personal finance
- Poor health
- Family tragedy
- Sex

77 **Safe conversational topics:**

- Sporting activities
- Cultural events
- Food and area restaurants
- Books
- Movies
- Vacation spots

78 **Beware these conversational train wrecks:**

- Asking about the family – no longer a safe topic
- Discussing your last surgery
- Dissing your ex-spouse
- Bemoaning your life's disappointments
- The weather – unless it's newsworthy
- Asking "What do you do?" since many executives may have been recently outplaced.

79 Stepping on (or interrupting) someone's sentences is as rude as stepping on their toes.

80 Repeatedly saying, "You know?" or "You know what?" is irritating.

81 Learn one interesting word a day! It will give you something of value to say.

*"Manners are a sensitive awareness
of the feelings of others.
If you have that awareness,
you have good manners,
no matter what fork you use."*
– Emily Post

YOUR PROFESSIONAL IMAGE

"Professionalism is knowing how to do it, when to do it ... and doing it."
– Frank Tyger

As we all have learned, the first impression is a lasting one. Many times the visual impression we make will cause someone to make judgments about us based on their perception, even before we speak.

Sounds like all the ingredients for paranoia, doesn't it? But, in fact, you reflect your company both internally and out in the community.

Even when traveling, people who might see the company logo on your luggage tag or take your business card will make judgments about you based on how you present yourself, both in dress and behavior. Take a look around you. True professionals are those who take a proactive approach. Notice how they are groomed and what they wear. Listen to their phone-answering messages. Look at their personal Web page, their posture, even the font they use in their e-mail responses. You'll find a proactive flavor in every aspect of their professional image.

And it's little things that count. It's the briefcase they carry, their choice of attire, even their tone of voice. Having a professional image must be habitually practiced 24/7.

Courtesy is contagious. Professionals know that how they treat others is as important as the last deal they brought to a successful result. They understand how their team members' progress is a direct reflection on their leadership.

"Whatever your level in the organization, business etiquette and interpersonal skills become even more important. Understanding business etiquette and applying them will go a long way to ensure success."

– Skip Walker, Retired CEO & Chairman, Hannah Corporation

82

Top Ten Ways to Enhance Your Professional Image:

- ✦ Return phone calls within 24 hours.
- ✦ Know your alcohol limit and don't exceed it.
- ✦ Keep your remarks positive.
- ✦ Ask to make a comment instead of interrupting the speaker.
- ✦ Turn away from gossip.

- Check for typos or poor grammar before sending letters, memos or e-mails.
- Keep complaints few and factual.
- Over-deliver rather than make empty promises.
- Catch yourself before you brag.
- Keep communication open with your boss and never allow him/her to be surprised or uninformed.

83 **If you want to be the boss, dress like one!**

- Appropriate to the situation.
- Pressed suits and casual clothing.
- Minimal and quality jewelry.

84 **Image spoilers:**

- Clothing too tight, wrinkled, soiled or needing repair.
- Skirt length or men's socks or slacks too short.
- Wearing perfume or cologne.
- Visible tattoos and facial piercings.
- Wearing low-cut blouses – no cleavage allowed!
- Stomach visible.
- Careless grooming – nails, cleanliness, breath, dandruff.

85 **Business casual comes in all shapes and sizes, but there are three specific levels:**

- *Base level* (those with no client contact) – jeans/khakis and knit shirts.
- *Mid level* – khakis or slacks, shirts with a collar, ties optional.
- *High level* – jacket, sweater, long-sleeve shirts and ties with slacks.

86 **What to wear when making a presentation:**

- ✦ Comfort is king. Wear clothing you feel good in.
- ✦ For a formal presentation, choose a pointed collar, long-sleeve shirt.
- ✦ Button-down shirts are fine for informal settings.
- ✦ Minimal jewelry.
- ✦ No dangling earrings.
- ✦ Medium- to dark-color suit is a better choice than black.
- ✦ Women can wear more colorful jacket/suit for keynotes.
- ✦ Serious presentations call for formal clothing. Keynotes or humorous speeches dictate more color.

87 Know and practice the rules of etiquette. A professional who knows etiquette and civility can handle any situation with ease and confidence.

88 **Act. Don't react.**

- ✦ Be a thermostat, not a thermometer.
- ✦ Never allow others to set your temperature for you.

89 **Business card etiquette:**

- ✦ Business cards define you. Use quality card stock and simple, easy-to-read information.
- ✦ When you are handed a business card, take the time to look at it carefully.
- ✦ Don't immediately stuff it away in a pocket or purse.
- ✦ Asking questions about the information on the card can be the starting point for insightful small talk.

90 Never force your business card on another person or interrupt them by offering your business card. Only offer your business card when you have engaged with someone and have reason to stay connected.

91 **Two ways to present your business card appropriately are:**

- After someone requests one.
- After you have asked permission to present one.

92 **When to use a business card:**

- Remind someone who you are and how to reach you.
- Attach to an article you are sending.
- Enclose with a business gift.

93 **Respect personal space:**

- When visiting another individual's office, protect and respect their personal space.
- Never put personal belongings on someone else's desk.
- Never touch anything on their desk unless you ask first or it is offered.

94 **Hints to help remember and recall names:**

- Concentrate on really hearing the person's name.
- Shake hands and maintain eye contact.
- Repeat the name aloud after you've been introduced.
- Use association techniques, e.g., knowing someone with the same name, visualizing a name like Sandy with the beach, etc.
- Write the name down at your first opportunity.

95

Always be considerate:

- ✦ Never keep a guest waiting.
- ✦ Greet visitors promptly upon their arrival.
- ✦ Don't overstay your welcome in another person's office.
- ✦ Acknowledge special occasions in a timely manner.

"As I grow older, I pay less attention to what people say. I just watch what they do."

– Andrew Carnegie

TECHNO-ETIQUETTE AND WRITTEN COMMUNICATIONS

"Technology makes it possible for people to gain control over everything ... except technology."
– John Tudor

In business today, it seems we're all "wired" and apparently enjoy being that way – or do we?

Witness the ringing cell phone at the last wedding ceremony or religious service you attended or the clicking of little fingers on PDAs at everything from convention presentations to football games. Or what about that person you just passed? Was he actually speaking to you, or did he have on an earpiece?

As early as the 1990s during the now infamous O.J. Simpson trial, we saw how electronic media can quickly invade any sacrosanct space. When attorney Robert Shapiro's cell phone rang the first time in Judge Ito's courtroom, he let it pass without comment. When the same phone barged into proceedings the second time, the judge threatened Shapiro with confiscation of the pesky little gadget.

Yes, we want to be wired … more in touch with friends, family, colleagues and clients. Yet, some psychologists are now reporting symptoms of cell phone and e-mail addiction. As we grow increasingly more dependent on electronics of every genre, let us not forget the importance of respect for others and their space, the value of face-to-face relationships and the very essence of humanity that has made this society one of the most dynamic in the history of the human race.

As early as the 1950s, scientist Albert Einstein remarked, "It is appallingly obvious that our technology has overtaken our humanity."

This would lead us to ask, "What would Einstein think of us now?"

TELEPHONE ETIQUETTE

96 Top Ten Telephone Do's and Taboos:

- Identify yourself and your company and move quickly to the point.
- Ask if the person has time to talk. If not, request a more convenient time.
- When leaving a phone message, state your name, company, day and time of your call, along with a callback number. Give your availability or ask for a telephone appointment convenient for them.

- Be clear and concise about the information you need in their return call.
- Ask permission before putting someone on hold.
- When answering for someone else, say, "May I ask who's calling?" rather than "Who is this?"
- Keep a notepad by the phone to document conversations.
- Summarize when closing the conversation.
- Never hang up after dialing a wrong number without apologizing.
- Transfer calls by explaining why the transfer is necessary, saying, "Miss Jones handles that area. Let me transfer you." Then tell Miss Jones the context of the call before transferring.

97

Put a smile in your voice. If it helps, keep a mirror at your desk.

98

Speak on the phone like you would speak to another person in the room. Use the same volume, speak clearly and slow enough for the other person to understand what you've said.

99

It's not productive to carry on a conversation and read e-mails at the same time. When communicating – using any media – it's more effective to focus on one task at a time.

100

Having a three-way call/conference call/speaker phone call? Here's how:

- Ask permission before placing a caller on speaker phone.
- Identify and inform everyone who is on the call.
- Be considerate and wait for the speaker to finish before you begin.

- ✦ Always identify yourself as you enter the conversation.
- ✦ Have the phone number handy in case of a dropped call.

101 **Handle complaints with class:**

- ✦ Listen and let the person talk. Don't interrupt!
- ✦ If you have the capability, be of help.
- ✦ If you can't handle the issue, transfer the call to someone who can.
- ✦ Never be defensive, rude or raise your voice.
- ✦ Tell the caller what you can do, then do it promptly.

102 **Administrative assistant tips when answering the phone:**

- ✦ Know how your boss prefers to have his/her phone answered.
- ✦ Offer a friendly greeting that includes the company name and your name while also capturing the spirit of the company.
- ✦ Don't over-screen! When you must ask for pertinent information, request it politely.
- ✦ Never say "Let me see if he's in." You should know if he is!

103 **When you must put your caller on hold:**

- ✦ Apologize, then ask permission.
- ✦ Permission denied? Take name and number and get back promptly!

104 Be punctual when providing additional information. Punctuality reflects professionalism.

105 On your voice mail message, provide information about when the caller can expect your call back.

106 Efficient communication is essential! Keep your staff informed of your schedule. This will prevent them from placing someone on hold, only to discover you're out of the office or in a meeting.

WRITTEN COMMUNICATIONS

107 The quality of your stationery is a direct reflection of you and your organization's image. Choose paper, design and printing carefully.

108 In written communications, use black ink. It reproduces with better clarity than blue ink.

109 **Don't just think it, ink it.**
When a letter of recommendation is requested, a thank-you note is needed or a letter of commendation has been earned, send one.

110 Send memos to inform and remind … especially yourself! Create and manage a to-do list.

111 **When writing a business letter, be brief:**

- Don't use slang.
- Write in short sentences – and write like you speak.
- Use a simple closing, such as "Sincerely."

112 Never address a letter to "Whom It May Concern" or "Dear Sir." Do the research required to find the name of the appropriate recipient.

WHEN USING E-MAIL, CELL PHONES, PDAs AND THE INTERNET:

113

Top 10 Tips for Effective E-mail:

- ✦ For sensitive issues, write the e-mail, think about it, then send it to yourself to re-read before actually sending it.
- ✦ Only use ALL CAPS for over-emphasizing. It's considered screaming.
- ✦ Summarize your content in the subject line.
- ✦ Keep paragraphs short. Consider using bullet points and/or subtitles if more than three paragraphs are necessary.
- ✦ Never send jokes, chain letters or personal pictures.
- ✦ Use business language.
- ✦ Use spell check … and then check again.
- ✦ Don't use acronyms. Spell words completely.
- ✦ Don't overuse the high-priority option.
- ✦ Acknowledge receipt of important information or attachments.

114

When working online:

- ✦ Respond, no matter what – except for junk mail.
- ✦ Get to the point.
- ✦ Use the address book function rather than listing all recipients.
- ✦ Re-read your messages to make sure there are no errors.
- ✦ If you only check e-mails once a week, let people know. If you don't, some may be put off because you are not sending timely answers.
- ✦ No gossiping, dissing others or providing details about the last office party online.
- ✦ Don't spend work time on personal online business, such as ordering Christmas gifts, etc.

- ✦ Avoid spam on your office e-mail account. Don't sign up for newsletters, free customer updates or flash reports.
- ✦ E-porn found on any office computer is usually grounds for immediate dismissal.
- ✦ If you leave a job and want to continue online relationships with customers and friends, notify them of your new work phone numbers, e-mail addresses and postal addresses.
- ✦ Use cc: field only when the recipient would know why they are receiving a copy.
- ✦ Use bcc: field when you don't want to disclose everyone's e-mail address to everyone else.

115 **Use cell phones respectfully.**

- ✦ Turn cell phones off or to vibrate when in public (where two or more are gathered for an activity).
- ✦ Keep them out of sight and don't take calls when having a conversation or attending a meeting.

116 Try not to discuss anything confidential in places where someone could eavesdrop, like on an airplane or in open spaces.

117 A simple ring tone is the best setting for your cell phone. Musical ring tones are annoying, particularly in a business setting.

118 When driving with a client or sharing a cab to the airport, don't get into an endless conversation. Those sharing small spaces with you have nowhere to hide. Don't subject them to your conversations!

119 Don't speak louder on your cell phone than you do on your landline. It's tasteless and unnecessary.

120 At a business lunch, don't place your cell phone next to your plate. Like a small tape recorder would inhibit your lunch conversation, your cell phone acts as an inhibitor as well.

121 Only wear one wireless device on your belt! Wearing your technology is not fashionable! It's like putting all your pens in your shirt pocket.

122 When conducting a cell phone conversation, 10 to 12 feet from another person is the acceptable proximity without invading their personal space.

123 Never dial your cell phone while driving. This activity is reserved only for those with a death wish!

124 Never talk on your cell phone in elevators, libraries, museums, restaurants, cemeteries, theaters, medical office waiting rooms, religious sites, auditoriums or other enclosed places, such as hospitals, courthouses, trains or buses.

125 **Faxes should not be used for:**

- Personal notes
- Confidential information
- Long material
- Junk mail

OFF-SITE BUSINESS MEETINGS

"Decide what your priorities are and how much time you'll spend on them. If you don't, someone else will."

– Harvey Mackay

How often do you attend a business meeting, convention or training seminar and, at the end, aren't too sure it was the best use of your time?

Like everything else, these events require some goal setting and planning before you go … as well as effort on your part to get the most out of every minute.

The following are some tips to help the next opportunity become more meaningful and successful for you:

126 Top Ten Ways to Prepare Before You Go:

- Stay at the meeting headquarters hotel in order to save travel time. Plus, you'll have more time for networking and meeting new people.
- Decide how you can benefit and what you can gain from the meeting. Think about your current goals (project goals, personal goals, career goals or goals for your team). Keep these in mind as you select workshops and seminars to attend.
- If you're attending with other members of your team, you may want to select seminars that cover areas of importance. Coordinate these selections with other attendees.
- Carry two functioning pens in your briefcase.
- Make a "key contacts" list – a list of people you want to connect with during the convention. Keep this list in your folder. If connecting with old friends, call or e-mail them in advance to set up social time together.
- Read about presenters. Learn about their backgrounds and special interests. List questions you'd like to ask, either during the presentation or afterward. Also list goals you'd like to meet while attending the presentation.
- Because some seminars and presentations are more popular than others, arrive 15 to 30 minutes early to assure yourself a seat up front.
- If the convention, workshop or meeting is financed by your organization, find out – before you leave – how expenses are to be reported. Get the necessary forms, making certain you keep a paper record of the expenses with original receipts.
- Make every minute count! Set expo priorities. Are there specific products you want to see? Any upgrades you want to know about for existing products? Write down booth numbers so you won't waste time searching for them.

- ✦ Maintain uninterrupted time for seminars and meetings by notifying clients and your office you will be unavailable during certain hours. This will keep you from running out of a seminar, just when the presenter is covering what you came to hear.

127 **Packing for the event:**

- ✦ Check the current weather and five-day forecast for the area you'll be visiting – then pack accordingly. Since weather has been known to turn on a dime, be prepared with rain gear, an extra jacket or sweater. And, remember, conventions are no place to break in new shoes.
- ✦ Take your chargers – for laptop, cell phone, PDA. In some cases, these tools will be doing double-duty, so make it easy by taking the necessary chargers along.
- ✦ Take an extra supply of business cards – and leave space in your backpack, briefcase or luggage for paperwork you'll collect during your meeting.
- ✦ Take a camera. Digital photos maintain connections long after the convention has ended.
- ✦ Pack an emergency kit that includes safety items, medicine, bandages, etc. You never know when you'll get an upset stomach, sore throat, etc. Be prepared with your own necessities.
- ✦ Take masking tape and safety pins for hems that may unravel, buttons that may pop, etc.

128 **Once you arrive:**

- ✦ Set a meeting spot for your team. Cell phones and PDAs may not be reliable in the convention or meeting areas, so plan in advance in case it's difficult to link up electronically.

- ✦ Be a "badge scanner." Look for networking opportunities as well as ways to begin conversations with other attendees.
- ✦ Determine to mix and mingle to meet new people. Don't "clump" with your buddies.
- ✦ Differentiate yourself. You might pass out a distinctive doodad that is representative of your company or your home state.
- ✦ One of the benefits of attending an outside meeting is to network and build relationships. Don't do all the talking. Keep the conversation going back and forth by asking open-ended questions and listening.
- ✦ During the seminars, you're there to listen and learn. So get involved, ask questions and share experiences when appropriate.
- ✦ Don't leave the room in the middle of a presentation. The speaker has spent time preparing for your benefit, so show respect. Likewise, your organization has spent money for you to attend.
- ✦ Keep an ongoing update of your activities, either by sending e-mails back to your office or maintaining a diary on your laptop. Every meeting, every seminar and every day will spawn new ideas you will want to follow up on when you get back.
- ✦ Call your office to check e-mails at least once a day. Return phone calls that might have been received during the time your cell phone was in the "vibrate" mode.
- ✦ Practice introducing yourself everywhere – to the person sitting next to you on the shuttle or the individuals standing around you when you're waiting in line. You never know what important person you'll meet.
- ✦ Have a conversation-starter speech prepared. For instance, "Hello, I'm Valerie Sokolosky and this is my first convention. What about you?"

- Use return travel time to summarize lessons learned and to capture new ideas.

129 When you get back to the office:

- Keep up the momentum. Make an action plan of the top three to five items you learned and want to follow up on. Make a timeline for implementation.
- Organize business cards you received and send a quick e-mail to each. If you have digital photos of these individuals, send them along.
- Send personal thank-you's to presenters you particularly enjoyed – and then keep in touch.
- Share and discuss what you've learned – through a brief meeting with your team or a roundup session with others who attended. Talk about what was the most important and applicable information from the conference. To make the meeting even more interesting, consider handing out mementos of the experience, such as apple seeds from Washington state, Mardi Gras beads from New Orleans, oranges from Florida or cotton bolls from a southern state.

130 To make the experience even more pleasant and productive:

- Practice moderation in everything, but particularly the use of alcohol. No seminar is ever good enough to beat that "hung over" feeling. And remember, your professional image is showing.
- Make allowances for time zone changes. If possible, go a day early and get your biorhythms back in sync.
- Maintain your personal activities schedule as much as possible. If you're an early riser, continue to rise early. If bedtime is

usually 9 p.m., go to bed about that same time. If you exercise daily, be sure to make time to do that, too.

- If you are not accustomed to a heavy diet, eat only foods you usually eat. Too many rich sauces, too much coffee or too many desserts often take their toll by the second or third day.
- Drink water. Stay hydrated, and be aware that alcohol and coffee dehydrate your body.
- Be extra aware of security. It's always better to travel in groups. Don't go anywhere you're not sure you will be safe, and watch your belongings.

131

Mind your (meeting) manners:

Do:

- Be present – in the moment.
- Think your ideas through before sharing them.
- Support your ideas with facts.
- Be open-minded to others' opinions.
- Take only your fair share of the meeting to contribute your ideas.
- Leave with a commitment to support the decisions made, no matter who presented the ideas.

Don't:

- Interrupt.
- Respond too quickly.
- Become defensive.
- Carry on side conversations.
- Attack opposing views.
- Belittle opposing ideas.
- Leave with a negative or uncooperative attitude.

WINE ETIQUETTE

"Etiquette means behaving yourself a little better than is absolutely essential."
– Will Cuppy

Traditionally, there has been a certain amount of snobbery surrounding the topic of wines … to the point that some people actually feel inadequate if they don't know much about wine.

Actually, just being aware of the basics will get you through most situations smoothly.

There are some, however, who feel the need to impress a client, a boss or a date with their ability to order and evaluate wines. Take heart. If you don't know the difference between a pinot noir and merlot, the following information will help.

When entertaining, find a good wine shop and an expert who will help you with choices and pairings for the food you plan to serve.

Remember: You're not expected to be a wine guru. When dining out, don't hesitate to ask for wine suggestions from the wine steward or waiter. That's their job!

132

Pairing wines with food:

Red Wines: Drink at room temperature with meats, fowl and cheeses.

White Wines: Drink chilled with white meat, light food and seafood.

Apertifs: Drink with munchies.

- ✦ Dry sherry
- ✦ Dry or sweet vermouth
- ✦ Dubonnet (red or white)
- ✦ Campari

Dessert Wines: Drink after dessert.

- ✦ Sauternes
- ✦ Sweet sherry
- ✦ Port
- ✦ Madeira

Sparkling Wines: Drink anytime, especially for celebrations.

- ✦ Asti Spumanti
- ✦ Schramsberg
- ✦ Champagne

After-Dinner Drinks: Drink after dinner when coffee is served.

- ✦ Port
- ✦ Cognac
- ✦ Armagnac
- ✦ Grappa
- ✦ Creme de menthe
- ✦ Cointreau
- ✦ Cream-finished liqueurs (Irish cream, creme de cacao)
- ✦ Peach-based cordials

133 **The general rules for ordering wine with a meal:**

- ✦ Most people tend to think a hearty, red wine (Bordeaux, burgundy or cabernet) is an appropriate complement to a red-meat meal, while white wine is best with white meat, fish or seafood.
- ✦ Dry white wines are also well-suited to pork and delicate dishes, such as sweetbreads.
- ✦ Sweet white wines are best with desserts.
- ✦ Red wines complement pâtés, beef, lamb, mutton, game and pasta dishes.
- ✦ Rosés are good with picnics, but typically not considered a savvy choice to order when dining out.
- ✦ Chicken, turkey, other poultry and veal are complemented by either red or white wines, except when served in a cream sauce, which calls for a dry white wine.
- ✦ Dry champagne is the one drink that complements all foods and is appropriate at any time.

134 During the course of a single meal, the traditional rule is to serve white wines before red wines, young wines before old wines, and dry wines before sweet wines. In other words, proceed from light wines to heavier ones.

135 **How wine will be served in a restaurant – and how you should respond:**

Step 1: The waiter/steward shows the bottle, label showing, to the person who ordered the wine … to make sure they brought what you ordered. Check the label, just to verify.

Step 2: The waiter opens the bottle and may hand you the cork or place it on the table. You have no obligation to sniff the cork, but if you decide to, make sure the bottom of the cork does not smell like mold or wet cardboard. If it does, politely decline the bottle.

Step 3: The waiter pours a small amount of wine for you to taste. This is yet another chance to determine if the wine is spoiled. To release the aroma of the wine, swirl the wine in the glass briefly. Or, you may skip it altogether, and ask the waiter to pour for everyone wishing wine at the table.

136 **What's corkage anyway?**

Some restaurants offer to serve the wine that a patron has brought, but will charge a corkage fee. However, this is not the case everywhere (especially on the East Coast).

Make certain you have called ahead to verify whether corkage is allowed.

Some restaurants will waive a corkage fee if an additional bottle is purchased from the wine list. To make sure of the policy, ask ahead of time.

After your waiter/sommelier opens and pours the contents of any wine you have brought to the restaurant, proper etiquette dictates you offer them a taste.

137 There are three tastes to every wine: the initial taste as the wine hits your palate, the secondary taste when the wine warms in the mouth and the aftertaste when you have swallowed the wine.

138 **For wine tasting at home:**

- ✦ Use the correct glasses for the wine being served.
- ✦ Serve the wine at proper temperature.
- ✦ Open red wines a bit before serving to let them "breathe."
- ✦ Cut the capsule (the foil just below the lip of the bottle).
- ✦ Don't bend the cork when uncorking.
- ✦ Make certain no bits of cork are floating in the wine.
- ✦ Pair food and wine to complement each other.

TRAVEL ETIQUETTE

"If you reject the food, ignore the customs,
fear the religion and avoid the people,
you might better stay home."
– James Michener

For many business professionals, the highways and skyways have become a "second home" of sorts, with travel requirements increasing, even in the wake of the well-connected communications networks within our global economy.

As customer bases become multinational and collaborative efforts more the rule than the exception, travel is now an essential part of many job descriptions – and the need to know how to "do the right thing" away from home has become as important as following domestic protocols.

Travel takes us from the familiar into the unfamiliar and from the comforts of home into the not-so-comfortable task of living away from home, family and friends.

Knowledge of travel etiquette has become as necessary as knowing how to read an itinerary or navigating one of the world's largest terminals. Being able to comfortably conduct oneself on airplanes is now as important for some professionals as driving turnpikes or freeways in the U.S.

Ultimately, as we travel, we not only represent our companies, but we also represent our country. Of course, there will be stereotypes. Being able to travel without causing discomfort to others or embarrassment to ourselves should always be the goal.

The following are basics that will help you travel professionally, while avoiding uncomfortable situations along the way.

139

Top Ten Tips to Fly High with Airplane Etiquette:

- When awaiting check-in, avoid cutting lines as if you have the right-of-way. You absolutely don't!
- Make it a habit to keep your seatbelt fastened, even when the overhead sign is off. You never know when a bump is coming!
- For your own safety and the safety of those around you, pay attention to flight attendants as they go through the pre-flight safety instructions. Pay attention to exit locations, how to use emergency oxygen and the location of flotation devices.
- Airplane etiquette violations can have serious consequences. Refrain from confrontations.
- Check excessive luggage or oversized bags. Most airlines are cracking down, and space is limited.

- ✦ Board quickly. Long conversations and taking your time at the entryway backs up traffic in the jet way.
- ✦ Once you're on the plane, get seated quickly to help traffic flow and "on time" departure.
- ✦ Over-the-shoulder luggage or backpacks should be carried in front of you as you make your way down the aisle. This avoids hitting passengers who are already seated.
- ✦ Take your reading materials out of your carry-on luggage before boarding the plane rather than fiddling with it in the aisle.
- ✦ Store your carry-on items under the seat in front of you or in the overhead bin adjacent to your seat. Don't put your bag in a bin near the front of the plane trying for a quick exit.

140 Never check your presentation materials, just in case your luggage gets lost.

141 Sit in your assigned seat.

142 If someone asks you to switch seats – and you're traveling alone – be a good neighbor and comply.

143 Don't hog the armrests.

144 When listening to music from your MP3 or video, don't crank up the sound.

145 Don't recline your seat all the way on a smaller plane. Remember, these are small spaces and you're taking legroom from the person behind you.

146 Always be considerate. The Golden Rule applies in the air, as well as on the ground.

147 On long flights, if you're more comfortable removing your shoes, use slipper socks.

148 Be considerate about seatmate conversations. There is nothing worse than being held captive by a talkative seatmate. This is not the place to discuss confidential business.

149 Sometimes nervous fliers use conversation to ease their fears. If you're bored or have work to do, excuse yourself from the conversation, but do it politely.

150 Don't wrench yourself out of your seat by grabbing the seat in front of you. Use your arm rests, instead.

151 Don't stand in front of the in-flight movie if there are no individual screens on your flight.

152 Don't stop and chat in the aisle.

153 Be careful when opening plastic dressing, condiment and beverage containers. They spatter easily. If you do spatter or spill something on someone, apologize and offer to pay for dry-cleaning.

154 An airliner's toilet is not a makeup table or dressing room. Be quick, and clean up after yourself.

155 An airline seat/tray table is not your office. Be neat.

156 Don't eavesdrop on your seatmate's conversation or attempt to read their book, work documents or laptop screen.

157 At the end of the flight, don't jump up and push your way to the door. Wait your turn. Proper exit flow is more efficient.

158 Be careful opening the bins. As the flight attendants warn, the contents do shift in flight.

159 If someone is having trouble getting his/her bag out of the overhead compartment, offer to help. It's a nice thing to do.

160 Standing in the jet way waiting for travel companions can cause a traffic jam. Wait to reassemble at the gate.

161 Don't stand behind a flight attendant working a cart, hoping it will, miraculously, disappear so you can get by.

162 Laptops should only take your "lap's space" on an airplane.

163 Remember – the airplane is a public place.

"Be prepared. If you don't know where you're going, you might end up somewhere else."

– Unknown

WORKING WITH PEOPLE WITH DISABILITIES

"It is a luxury to be understood."
– Ralph Waldo Emerson

According to the National Organization on Disability, approximately 54 million Americans are living with some type of disability.

The Americans with Disabilities Act (ADA) was developed with the goal of integrating people with disabilities into all aspects of American life, particularly the workplace and the marketplace.

It's important to remember, individuals with physical disabilities who need special conveyances may have graduated at the top of their class. Don't dismiss those who don't look like you as being limited. In fact, they may offer amazing contributions to your business and your workforce.

When supervisors and co-workers are sensitive and respectful toward those with disabilities, these individuals feel more comfortable, are more productive and have a stronger commitment to the team.

Never feel awkward when meeting or working with someone who has a disability. If you're unsure what to do or say, just ask – they'll tell you.

In the meantime, the following tips are not only worth knowing, they're also worth sharing.

Remember, we're all the same. We're all people – we just have different talents and abilities.

164

Top Ten Tips for Working With Those With Disabilities:

- Just because someone has a disability doesn't mean they need help. Offer assistance only if the person appears to need help. And if they do want help, ask how before you act.
- Never pat someone with disabilities on the head or touch their wheelchair, scooter or cane. This is their private space. If you need to move them, ask for permission.
- Speak directly to the individual with the disability – not to their companion, aide or sign language interpreter.
- When introduced to someone with a disability, offer to shake hands. People with limited hand use or who wear artificial

limbs usually can shake hands. It is perfectly permissible to offer your left hand.

- When shaking hands, remember some people – and it isn't often visible – may have joint problems in their hands. A firm but not crushing grip will be less painful for these individuals.
- When talking to someone seated in a wheelchair or scooter for any length of time, place yourself at their eye level – to avoid stiff necks and "talking down" to the individual.
- Remember to keep your face visible when speaking to someone who is deaf or hard of hearing. They may be relying on reading your lips.
- Don't shout or raise the volume of your voice unless asked to do so.
- When greeting someone who is blind or has a visual impairment, identify yourself and who may be accompanying you.
- Never touch or pet a service dog or make the dog the focus of your conversation. Their dog is "working."

165 When interacting with a person who is visually impaired, follow their lead. If they need assistance, they will ask.

166 Allow the person to negotiate their surroundings, such as finding the door handle, locating a chair, etc.

167 Treat adults as adults. Address people with disabilities by their first name only when extending the same familiarity to others.

168 People with disabilities are comfortable with children's natural curiosity and do not mind if a child asks them questions about their circumstances.

169 People who have disabilities are the best judges of what they can or cannot do. Don't make assumptions for them about participating in various activities.

170 When people with disabilities ask for an accommodation at your business, it is not a complaint. It shows they feel comfortable enough to ask for what they need.

171 When referring to someone with a disability, say, "person with a disability" rather than "disabled person." Say, "the woman who is deaf," not "the deaf woman."

172 Avoid outdated terms, such as "handicapped" or "crippled."

173 People who use crutches or canes need their arms to balance themselves, so it's not a good idea to grab them in any way.

174 People who are mobility-impaired often lean on a door for support. So pushing the door open from behind or unexpectedly opening the door may cause them to fall.

175 If a new employee or customer is blind or visually impaired, offer to take them on a tour of your facility. As you tour, describe the setting and note obstacles, such as stairs, large cracks in sidewalks and other hazards.

176 People who are blind need their arms for balance, so offer your arm – don't take theirs – if they need to be guided.

177 If a person with visual impairment uses a service dog, walk on the side opposite the dog.

178 If you serve food to a person who is blind, describe what is on the plate and where. Remove anything inedible, such as garnishes.

179 Some need their food cut up, particularly meat portions. Request this to be done in the kitchen before the meal is served.

180 People who are deaf need to be included in decisions affecting them. Don't decide for them.

181 A TTY is a small device with a keyboard, a paper printer or visual display screen and acoustic couplers for a telephone receiver. When a TTY caller calls your business, the operator will identify the call as such. This way, people who are deaf are able to communicate with your business.

182 There are more than 200 growth-related disorders. Never pet or kiss a person of short stature on the head.

183 Communication is easier when people are on the same physical level. Sit in a chair when speaking to someone of shorter stature.

184 Remember, not all disabilities are obvious. If an employee or customer makes a specific request, do your best to comply and respect that individual's needs.

185 The Americans with Disabilities Act requires every business, regardless of size or mission, to provide access to people with disabilities. This is federal law.

According to the U.S. Department of Labor, the percentage of people with disabilities aged 16-64 employed is 55.8%, which represents 23% of the work force.

SPECIAL TOPICS

"Tact is...'giving the other fellow
the sense of ease in one's presence.'"
– Gordon Lindsay

We've included this section to cover those situations and events that are common to everyone.

Sometimes, these instances are uncomfortable and, many times, embarrassing. So we have offered the "best practices" for those times when we are unsure of what to say or do.

If you're not comfortable with our suggestion, we encourage you to go with your intuition, gut feeling or your good common sense.

186 **After a death, express sympathy simply and genuinely.**
Here's what grief specialist Doug Manning suggests – called the **3 H's:**

- *Hang around* – Find out if the family has any needs, such as answering the phone, cleaning bathrooms or getting meals prepared. Don't "camp" at the home of the survivors, unless they request it.
- *Hold 'em* – Sometimes individuals just like to sit with someone quietly or may just need a hug. Don't force yourself in any situation, but be sensitive and aware of the individual's needs, e.g., to rest, to eat or drink, or just to be alone.
- *Hush* – Your presence speaks volumes. You don't have to say anything. Certainly avoid making trite statements, such as "Time heals all wounds."

187 When you see an unsightly piece of food stuck between another's teeth or on their face, simply tell them, "I think you have something on your cheek you'll want to remove."

188 A co-worker's tendency to overuse perfume can be pointed out by saying, "I'm sure you're not aware, but your perfume is over-powering and several of us have allergies to any perfume and cologne. I thought you would want to know so it doesn't cause you a problem."

189 When someone has body odor or bad breath, first recognize that most people would want to know. If you decide to tell the person, do it privately and tactfully by saying something like, "Marie, as a friend I'm sure you would want to know something that is difficult for me to share. You probably are not aware that your breath is stale. It may be caused by a health issue, and I wanted to let you

know so that you can do something about it." Usually, the individual is unaware, and most of us would want to know. *Note*: Both of these may be symptoms of a health problem.

190 When you see a blouse unbuttoned, a fly open or a piece of lettuce between teeth, DO tell. Be sensitive, inconspicuous and gracious. Again, most of us would appreciate being told and able to quickly resolve the situation.

191 When it's time to leave – a job or a relationship – say goodbye graciously. Burning bridges only narrows future opportunities. Keep the negatives to yourself, be appreciative for past positives and move on.

192 Upon receipt of an unexpected gift, your only obligation is to be sincere in your thanks at the time – and in a follow-up, handwritten thank-you note. Remember, one gift does not necessarily deserve another.

"When you want to be honored by others,
you learn to honor them first."
– Sathya Sai Baba

INTERNATIONAL ETIQUETTE

"Those who know nothing of foreign languages know nothing of their own."
– Johann Wolfgang von Goethe

As business has become more global, traveling abroad – once a luxury for American business – is now a necessity. And because so much U.S. business activity now depends on international relationships, it's more important than ever before to know what's expected – and respected – when doing business in other countries.

Yet, Americans still often fly abroad and meet international business people with nothing more than a proposal in hand, a briefcase full of information and perhaps a short briefing from their company as to what should be accomplished. Then they are surprised when a promising international deal collapses, seldom with any explanation as to what went wrong.

While Americans are getting more sophisticated about doing business internationally, we still have a long way to go in becoming more globally sensitive and in effectively building relationships with other cultures. Only then can we move, comfortably and successfully, from the dining table to the executive boardroom in making deals anywhere in the world.

Cultural sensitivity doesn't mean just learning a few phrases for the language and some details about a particular country. It's more about the three A's – attitude, awareness and adaptation – to the ways other cultures do business.

People do business with people they know and trust, and with whom they feel comfortable.

Several Asian cultures take this sentiment even further with the age-old proverb:

Relationships first, business second.

More international business deals have been lost because of the way in which someone conducted business than because of language barriers or any problem with the business itself. This chapter is a good starting point in assuring not only your cultural savvy, but also the most respectful and cordial conduct when working with other nationalities.

193 **Top Ten Tips Traveling Abroad:**

- ✦ Use complete title when making introductions. Learn to pronounce your international host's or guest's name correctly.
- ✦ Take ample supply of business cards. Exchanging them is a ritual in many countries. Wait until your host offers his/her card or asks for yours, and then offer it. Take time to look at a card when it is presented. Treat the card respectfully once you receive it, e.g., don't write on it, fold it or put it in your pocket and sit on it. These actions can be taken as an insult in some countries.
- ✦ Use simple, easily understandable language. Avoid regional expressions or idioms like "y'all" or "dude." These are rarely understood and can lead to serious misunderstandings.
- ✦ Learn a few phrases of the local language, especially "please," "thank you," and "nice to meet you."
- ✦ Don't carry an extra set of psychological baggage, e.g., "cultural baggage." Avoid pre-conceived notions and stereotypes about other cultures.
- ✦ Develop an appropriate attitude that we, as Americans, are ambassadors for not only our companies, but also for our country and our way of life.
- ✦ Use the word "nationalities" rather than "foreigners" to describe those from other cultures.
- ✦ Plan carefully. Arrive in time to recover from jet lag so you are fresh and rested for the meeting. And give yourself plenty of time to get to appointments, especially in large, crowded cities such as Tokyo, Mexico City, Paris, Rome, Hong Kong, and London. Be on time, and respect the agenda that your hosts may have prepared or suggest.

- ✦ Learn about the country's institutions, social classes, dress codes, language, political system, religious beliefs, values and attitudes, greetings and gestures.
- ✦ Don't be too casual or abrupt. Err on the side of formality. In most other countries, people address each other formally until they get to know you well. Even in the cases where you know a business colleague or client well, you would still want to err on the side of a formal address unless the person tells you to use the informal address.

194 Dress conservatively unless you know that a particular country's dress code is more casual.

195 Women should avoid pants, short skirts and sleeveless dresses, since some countries, such as the Middle East, consider such attire an affront to their beliefs and customs. Be advised that in Latin America, it's more common for women to wear clothing that Americans might consider suggestive, and at the very least, evening wear. You may not want to wear this kind of clothing, but don't be alarmed if you see Latin American women doing so at trade shows and other business events.

196 Asians may remove their shoes and even their sunglasses before entering homes. You should do the same to respect their culture.

197 In Europe, don't take off your suit coat in restaurants, offices or on the street. Follow your host's lead.

198 Don't display too much "rugged individualism" or blatant competitiveness. Seventy percent of the world's cultures have more of a group orientation in all areas of their lives than Americans do.

199 Do be patient. Keep in mind that time is a different concept in many other parts of the world. On the other hand, be punctual for meetings in Asia and Europe. In Spain, India and Latin America, being late is considered normal. Be sure you determine how "late" is considered acceptable. In some places it is an hour; in other places it is half an hour.

200 Discussing family in Arab countries is taboo.

201 Don't give a firm handshake in China, Saudi Arabia, France or Japan. Notice, too, that Hispanics, Greeks and Germans shake hands repeatedly. French people shake hands with average (compared to most Americans) firmness and do so repeatedly. For example, it is normal to shake hands with all of your colleagues every day upon the first encounter of the day, even if you work regularly with them and see them daily. This is the custom even if the first encounter happens toward the end of the day. It's also not unusual in an afternoon meeting to shake hands with the people you are seeing for the first time that day and not with those with whom you have shaken hands earlier in the same day.

202 During meetings in China, body language counts. Stay calm, collected and controlled.

203 In China, establish a contact to act as in intermediary who can serve as an informant to you on customs and procedures, as well as be an interpreter to help with the bureaucracy and legal system.

204 In Japan, receive a business card with both hands saying "thank you." Then, study the card for a few seconds before putting it in a jacket or card case. If you are seated at a table, do not put the card away. Lay it in front of you.

205 Have your business card printed in English on the front and the other country's most common language on the reverse. But, make sure that the translation is checked by a native speaker to avoid any embarrassment due to misinterpretation by the translator.

206 Know which name (first or last) is correct to use when addressing someone.

207 Topics of conversation should avoid anything in the way of personal information or questions. *Exception*: in Latin American countries, family is a major topic of discussion.

208 Don't shout at people from other cultures. Americans tend to raise their voices when conversing, a habit that is rude, particularly to the generally soft spoken Asian colleague.

209 Use concrete words and be as specific as possible. Speak slowly and clearly. Avoid telling jokes and using slang or jargon in either verbal or written communication. Humor does not translate well. Neither do figures of speech and buzzwords. Use words that can't

be misinterpreted. For instance, you might get a puzzled look when suggesting that you and an international client "paint the town red," that you have arranged a great "dog and pony show," or that your product supplies a lot of "bang for your buck."

210 Do become comfortable with silence. People in many cultures, such as Japan, use silence to collect their thoughts. Learn to sit quietly. It will be perceived as a sign of strength when you are in the midst of a difficult negotiation.

211 Be cautious with lavish compliments. Middle Easterners enjoy giving and receiving praise, but some cultures look upon excessive compliments suspiciously. Others feel compelled to give you, as a gift, some possession of theirs you have verbally admired.

212 Check to make sure you are being understood. In Japan, business people frequently nod, smile, and say "yes" (hai) to be polite. That doesn't mean that the other person agrees with or understands everything that you say. In Bulgaria and Greece, a nod actually means "no."

213 Do invite questions when you make a presentation. But don't be surprised if, in Japan for example, no one asks anything until you have completed your presentation. Be sure to summarize your talk to make sure you get the main points across.

214 The Chinese have a reputation for being tough negotiators. Be aware that their main concern in negotiations is "concessions." Be willing to compromise. And recognize that decisions often take a long time.

215 Don't interrupt another person. Almost all cultures consider this rude.

216 Don't back away if someone from another culture stands close when talking. People from Hispanic countries and Middle Eastern men tend to stand very close and may touch your arm or shoulder when speaking. Business men in Mexico frequently pat each other on the back or embrace each other in an *abrazo*, or hug. The first time this happens it might startle an American man, but receiving an abrazo is an honor and means that you're accepted and trusted. People from most Asian countries, however, have been brought up to give as much space to other people as possible. They may stand farther apart and avoid touching others.

217 Watch cultural differences in the way people make eye contact. Asians may avoid eye contact as a sign of respect, while Middle Eastern males maintain very direct eye contact. It is all right for you to continue your customary practice, but be careful not to misinterpret cultural differences as either lack of attention or as aggressiveness.

218 Avoid hand gestures, such as beckoning with upturned finger, which is offensive in Asian countries because this is how animals are called – snapping your fingers, making "okay" signs, or pointing with a finger. These gestures can be interpreted as rude or even obscene in many countries. Arab countries consider it highly offensive to use the left hand for any kind of gesture – eating or touching – since this is the hand reserved for personal hygiene.

219 Maintain good posture and formal body position, e.g., crossing your leg over your other knee.

220 Don't lean on an arm, yawn, stretch, or slouch. These are universal signs of boredom and inattentiveness.

221 Don't put your hands in your pockets, especially during presentations. This too-casual, indifferent gesture is especially offensive in German, Austrian and Scandinavian cultures.

222 With gestures, a good rule of thumb is "when in doubt, don't" – even if you have to sit on your hands for fear of making a mistake.

223 Write thank-you notes and letters to your hosts after an international trip. Write clearly and formally.

224 Don't assume you can use laptop computers, faxes, cell phones or even the telephone in the same manner as in the United States; confirm in advance that you can do so through your hotel or another location.

225 Confirm appointments, and plan to conduct most of your business in person in countries where the phone system is not state-of-the-art.

226 Sample the local cuisine before the trip to prepare yourself for foods that may be unusual to you.

227 Carefully research the gift-giving customs in a particular country before you present or receive a gift. Gift-giving is an area where errors are common. The Japanese, for example, expect and like to receive gifts, especially frozen steaks, which are expensive in their

country. But take care not to give gifts in multiples of four, e.g., four pens, as the number is associated with death.

228 Know if you should open a gift in front of the giver in the country you are visiting. Customs also dictate how gifts should be wrapped and presented.

229 In China, business gifts are reciprocated, e.g., they are seen as debts needing to be repaid. Always select gifts of worth and beauty, never money.

230 Err in the direction of giving elaborate gifts in Arab countries, modest gifts in Japan and obvious logo gifts in certain European countries.

231 In general, avoid giving gifts at a first business meeting. It may be interpreted as a bribe (except in Japan).

INTERNATIONAL GIFT GIVING/RECEIVING

Buying Abroad for Colleagues, Family Members, and Friends:

232 Know the country's specialties in advance to make ideal purchases.

233 Know the international size differences. Dress and shirt sizes may not translate.

234 Take a picture of the person you're buying for standing next to you to size them up for what size they would wear.

235 Shop in the region's shopping district, where there are usually better selections.

236 Most business gifts for personal use may be included within your customs exemptions. Large quantities of gifts intended for business, promotional or other commercial purposes may or may not be included.

237 Suggested gifts that are most appropriate include spices, cooking utensils, cookbooks, art and antiques, books and music, golf and sporting items or gifts "made in America" if giving abroad.

238 Take a gift if you are invited to someone's home.

239 Flowers and quality chocolates are appropriate in Europe and Japan. In many parts of Europe, wine is acceptable.

240 Gifts that spell trouble include food, plants, shells and money.

241 When taking a gift abroad, wait until you arrive to wrap it.

242 Avoid white, black or brown wrapping paper in Germany.

243 Give attention to the presentation of the gift. Present the gift in person. If you can't, then make sure a note accompanies the item and follow up with a phone call.

244 Sign and date the gift. Let the recipient know if there's a story that goes along with the item purchased, or if directions are necessary.

245 These tips for gift-giving and receiving should smooth the way to social graces abroad. The following ideas will help you decide what gifts you'd like to bring back for yourself or others that are particularly germane to the country listed.

INTERNATIONAL PURCHASING IDEAS	
Australia	Black opals, boomerangs, stuffed animals, scenic books, woolen blankets, fine coffees, coral and jade, fine chocolates.
China	Linen, lace, name art, porcelain
Hong Kong	Jewelry, linens, cloisonné ware, pearls
Japan	Silk, art, mother of pearl, dolls, china, porcelain, batik, lacquered bowls
Malaysia	Tin, spices
New Zealand	Sheep skin, hats, highland music, scenic books
Philippines	Wicker, rattan, teak wood
South Korea	Eel skin, clothing, Caledon, copy paintings
Singapore	Silk, cloisonné ware, batik, pewter, 22k gold
Taiwan	Rugs, lace, cloisonné ware
Thailand	Jewelry, silk, pearls, gold, rubies, rare spices, pottery
Europe	Antique jewelry, jewels, fine leather, books, fine silver, perfumes, oils
Russia	Nesting dolls, fine artifacts
Mexico	Blankets, pottery, jewelry
Caribbean	Shells, fossils, baskets, bags
Hawaii	Gold jewelry, diamonds, bags, onions, pineapples, Kona coffee
Canada	Furs, coffees, fine leather goods
Alaska	Smoked salmon, fine leather goods, furs

Valerie Sokolosky is a nationally recognized author and speaker on professionalism in the workplace. In addition to authoring seven books, Valerie is currently President of Valerie & Company, a certified, woman-owned leadership development firm based in Dallas, TX. During the past 25 years, her firm has received front-page *Wall Street Journal* press coverage, and she has been quoted as an expert in her field in *The Washington Post* and *Glamour* magazine, among others. She is Publisher for *Women's Enterprise* national news magazine and was a monthly contributor for ten years in Southwest Airlines' *Spirit* magazine.

Valerie has held several leadership positions where these business etiquette issues surface frequently. She served as Vice-Chairman of the Board of the prestigious organization Leadership America, as well as currently holding a board position on Executive Women of Dallas. She has been honored as Delta Zeta Woman of the Year, participated in M.I.T. President's Forum, and is listed as Who's Who of Women Executives.

Her firm provides keynotes, executive coaching and training (interpersonal skills, management development, professional image and business etiquette) to many Fortune 500 companies, including Verizon, Deloitte, AMD, American Airlines, Dell Computers, EDS, Microsoft, Shell Oil, Texaco, Neiman-Marcus, Motorola, United States Air Force Protocol Office, NASA, State Farm, Pfizer, ConAgra, McKesson, Federal Reserve Bank, Georgia Pacific, St. Joseph's Hospital, Baylor Health Care, DuPont, KPMG, Mary Kay, SHRM, MPI, and Halliburton, among others.

Valerie is also the author of *Monday Morning Leadership for Women,* an Amazon.com best-seller about a manager and her mentor. It provides insights and wisdom on how to deal with leadership issues that are unique to women.

For more information about Valerie & Company, please visit **www.valerieandcompany.com.**

To book Valerie Sokolosky for a speaking engagement, please call 214-290-0100.

Accelerate Personal Growth Resources

12 Choices…That Lead to Your Success is about success…how to achieve it, keep it and enjoy it…by making better choices. $14.95

Orchestrating Attitude translates the incomprehensible into the actionable. It cuts through the clutter to deliver inspiration and application so you can orchestrate your attitude…and your success. $9.95

Conquering Adversity – Six Strategies to Move You and Your Team Through Tough Times is a practical guide to help people and organizations deal with the unexpected and move forward through adversity. $14.95

107 Ways to Stick to It What's the REAL secret to success? Learn the secrets from the world's highest achievers. These 107 practical, inspiring tips will help you stick to it and WIN! $9.95

The Ant and the Elephant is a different kind of book for a different kind of leader! A great story that teaches that we must lead ourselves before we can expect to be an effective leader of others. $12.95

Too Many Emails contains dozens of tips and techniques to increase your email effectiveness and efficiency. $9.95

175 Ways to Get More Done in Less Time has 175 really good suggestions that will help you get things done faster…usually better. $9.95

Becoming the Obvious Choice is a roadmap showing each employee how they can maintain their motivation, develop their hidden talents, and become the best. $9.95

You and Your Network is profitable reading for those who want to learn how to develop healthy relationships with others. "I think every living person should read and re-read this book. It can change your life." – David Cottrell $9.95

136 Effective Presentation Tips is a powerful handbook providing 136 practical, easy to use tips to make every presentation a success. $9.95

Silver Bullets contains straightforward tips on how to gain success while keeping your wits about you. $14.95

The NEW CornerStone Perpetual Calendar, a compelling collection of quotes about leadership and life, is perfect for office desks, school and home countertops. $14.95

CornerStone Collection of Note Cards Sampler Pack is designed to make it easy for you to show appreciation for your team, clients and friends. The awesome photography and your personal message written inside will create a lasting impact. Pack of 12 (one each of all 12 designs) $24.95

Visit www.**CornerStoneLeadership**.com for additional books and resources.

☑ **YES! Please send me extra copies of *Do It Right!***
1-30 copies $14.95 31-100 copies $13.95 101+ copies $12.95

Do It Right! ____ copies X ______ = $ ______

Additional Personal Growth Resources

Accelerate Personal Growth Package ____ pack(s) X $139.95 = $ ______
(Includes one each of all items listed on page 94.)

Other Books

______________________ ____ copies X ______ = $ ______

______________________ ____ copies X ______ = $ ______

______________________ ____ copies X ______ = $ ______

______________________ ____ copies X ______ = $ ______

______________________ ____ copies X ______ = $ ______

Shipping & Handling $ ______

Subtotal $ ______

Sales Tax (8.25%-TX Only) $ ______

Total (U.S. Dollars Only) $ ______

Shipping and Handling Charges

Total $ Amount	Up to $49	$50-$99	$100-$249	$250-$1199	$1200-$2999	$3000+
Charge	$6	$9	$16	$30	$80	$125

Name ______________________ Job Title ______________

Organization ______________________ Phone ______________

Shipping Address ______________________ Fax ______________

Billing Address ______________________ E-mail ______________
(required when ordering PowerPoint® Presentation)

City ______________________ State __________ ZIP ______________

❑ Please invoice (Orders over $200) Purchase Order Number (if applicable) ______________

Charge Your Order: ❑ MasterCard ❑ Visa ❑ American Express

Credit Card Number ______________________ Exp. Date ______________

Signature ______________________________________

❑ Check Enclosed (Payable to: CornerStone Leadership)

Fax
972.274.2884

Mail
P.O. Box 764087
Dallas, TX 75376

Phone
888.789.5323

www.**CornerStoneLeadership**.com

Thank you for reading *Do It Right!*
We hope it has assisted you in your quest for personal and professional growth.

CornerStone Leadership is committed to provide new and enlightening products to organizations worldwide. Our mission is to fuel knowledge with practical resources that will accelerate your team's productivity, success and job satisfaction!

Best wishes for your continued success.

CornerStone
Leadership Institute
www.CornerStoneLeadership.com

Start a crusade in your organization –
have the courage to learn, the vision to lead,
and the passion to share.